THE YOUNG FLUTIST'S RECITAL BOOK

Three Centuries of Flute Music
selected from the
Louis Moyse Collection

ED-3457

G. SCHIRMER, Inc.

DISTRIBUTED BY

HAL•LEONARD®
CORPORATION

7777 W. BLUEMOUND RD. P.O. BOX 13819 MILWAUKEE, WI 53213

CONTENTS

SONATA No. 4

Realization of the figured bass
by Louis Moyse

Johann Sebastian Bach
(1685-1750)

* All trills should start on the
note above and on the beat.

48597cx

Allegro

Menuett I

Menuett II

Da capo Menuett I

CANTABILE
Second Movement from Concerto in D, Op. 10, No. 3

Antonio Vivaldi
(1669-1741)

48597

TWO PASSEPIEDS
from Suite in A minor

I

Georg Philipp Telemann
(1681-1767)

Fine

II

Passepied I D.C. senza replica

SONATINA in F

Georg Philipp Telemann
(1681-1767)

I

II

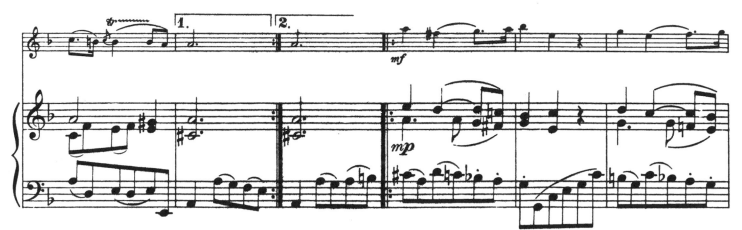

III

15

48597

SERENADE

Franz Joseph Haydn
(1732-1809)

Andante cantabile ♩= c. 108

ADAGIO
from Quartet, K.285

Wolfgang Amadeus Mozart
(1756-1791)

48597

Flute

THE YOUNG FLUTIST'S RECITAL BOOK

CONTENTS

ED-3457

G. SCHIRMER, *Inc.*

DISTRIBUTED BY

HAL•LEONARD® CORPORATION

7777 W. BLUEMOUND RD. P.O. BOX 13819 MILWAUKEE, WI 53213

SONATA No. 4

Johann Sebastian Bach
(1685-1750)

*All trills should start on the note above and on the beat.

All dots and dashes written under or at the end of a slur indicate the note should be tongued.

48597cx

4

Adagio

p espressivo

mp

cresc.

f

p

cresc. *molto* *rit.* *f*

Menuett I

p

mp *poco cresc.* *mf*

Menuett II

p dolce

p

cresc. *mf*

pp *cresc.*

mf

Da capo Menuett I

48597

CANTABILE
Second Movement from Concerto in D, Op. 10, No. 3

Antonio Vivaldi
(1669-1741)

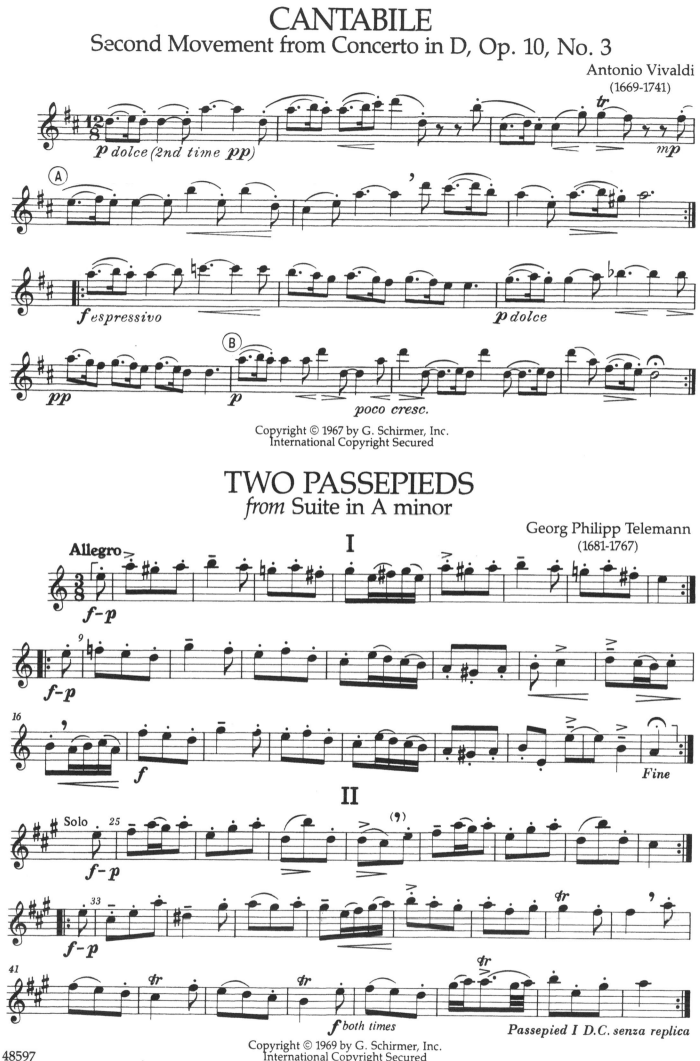

p dolce (2nd time pp)

mp

A

f espressivo

p dolce

B

pp

p

poco cresc.

Copyright © 1967 by G. Schirmer, Inc.
International Copyright Secured

TWO PASSEPIEDS
from Suite in A minor

Georg Philipp Telemann
(1681-1767)

I

Allegro

f-p

f-p

f

Fine

II

Solo

f-p

f-p

f both times

Passepied I D.C. senza replica

Copyright © 1969 by G. Schirmer, Inc.
International Copyright Secured

SONATINA in F

I

Georg Philipp Telemann
(1681-1767)

II

Cantabile

III

Presto

SERENADE

Franz Joseph Haydn
(1732-1809)

ADAGIO
from Quartet, K.285

Wolfgang Amadeus Mozart
(1756-1791)

ALLEGRO
from Sonata in A

Wolfgang Amadeus Mozart
(1756-1791)

* Before the beat

POLONAISE
from Sonata in B♭

Ludwig van Beethoven
(1770-1827)

MOMENT MUSICAL

Franz Schubert
(1797-1828)

Allegro moderato ♩ = c. 84

ROMANZE

Robert Schumann
(1810-1856)

Semplice, affettuoso

ANDANTE CON MOTO

Johannes Brahms
(1833-1897)

REVERIE

Claude Debussy
(1862-1918)

Dreamily

48597

GYMNOPÉDIE

Erik Satie
(1866-1925)

Lento e tristo

ALLEGRO
from Sonata in A

Wolfgang Amadeus Mozart
(1756-1791)

(Allegro)

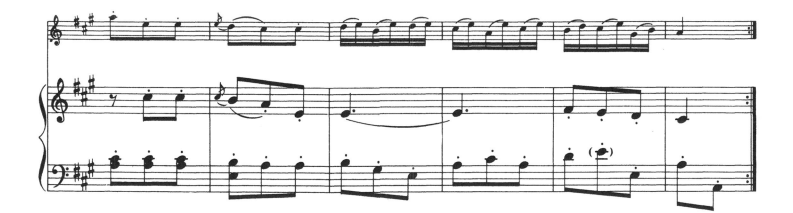

* Before the beat

48597

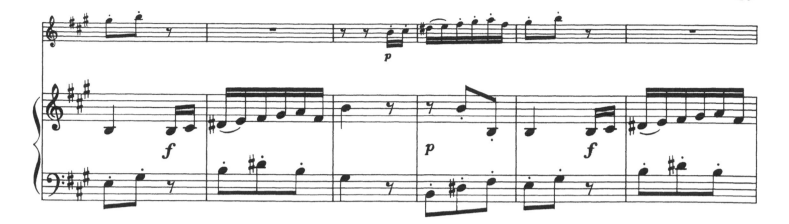

48597

48597

POLONAISE
from Sonata in B♭

Ludwig van Beethoven
(1770-1827)

Trio

MOMENT MUSICAL

Franz Schubert
(1797-1828)

Allegro moderato ♩ = c. 84

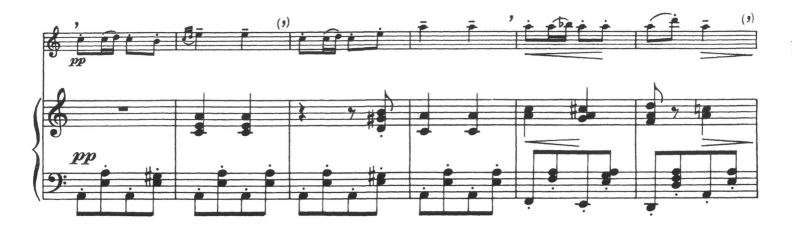

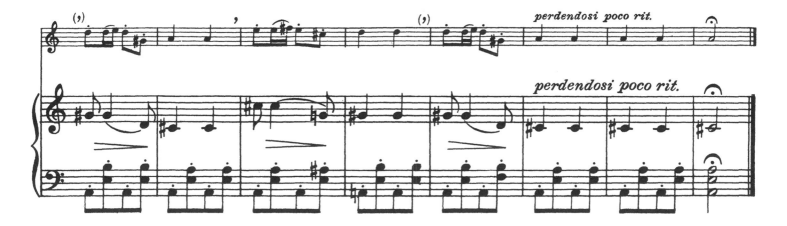

ROMANZE

Robert Schumann
(1810-1856)

Simplice, affettuoso

48597

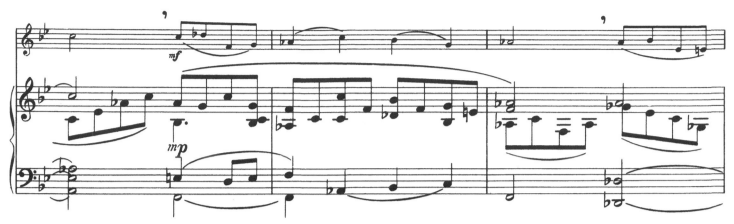

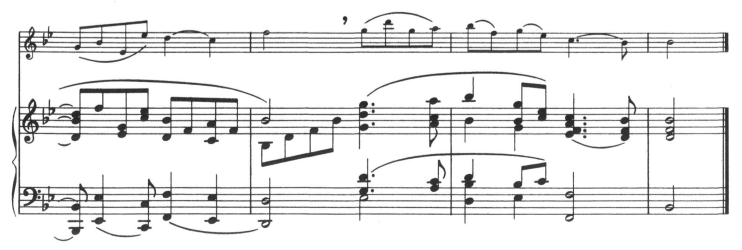

ANDANTE CON MOTO

Johannes Brahms
(1833-1897)

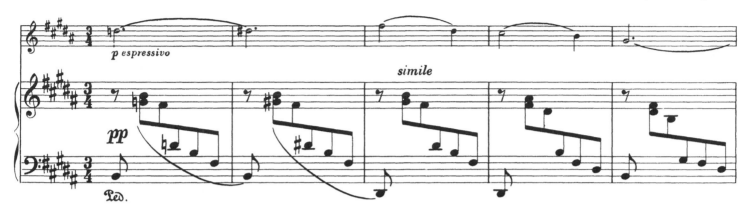

REVERIE

Claude Debussy
(1862-1918)

Tempo I

GYMNOPÉDIE

Erik Satie
(1866-1925)

Lento e tristo

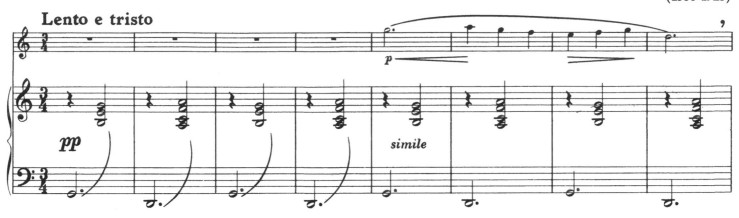

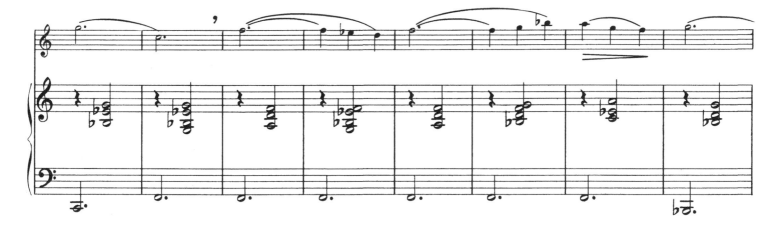

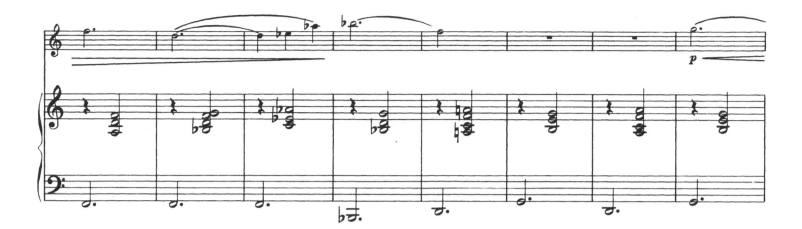

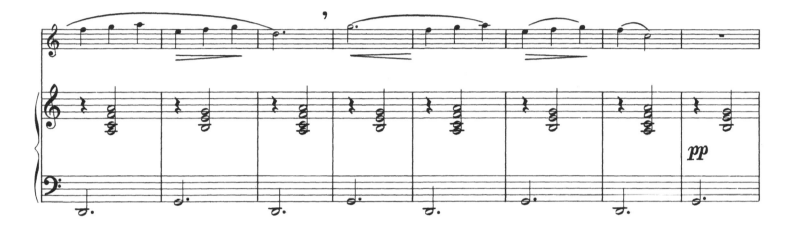

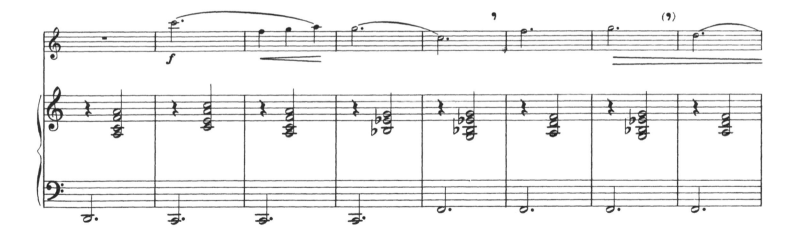

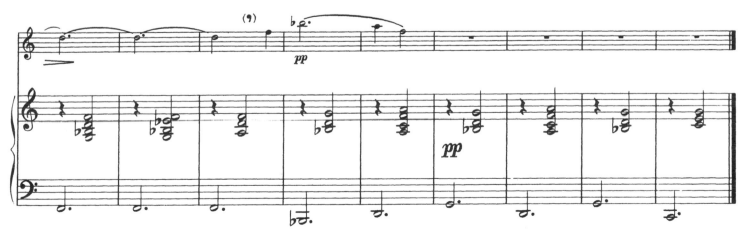